Little Prayers

for

EVERYDAY
LIFE

28 27 26 25 24 23 22   1 2 3 4 5 6 7 8

Hardcover ISBN: 978-1-5064-6880-8
eBook ISBN: 978-1-5064-7140-2

Library of Congress Cataloging-in-Publication Data

Names: Smith, Traci, 1978- author. | Jones, Anna, 1977- illustrator.
Title: Little prayers for everyday life / by Traci Smith ; illustrated by
    Anna Jones.
Description: Minneapolis, MN : Beaming Books, [2022] | Audience: Ages 3-5 |
    Summary: "An illustrated prayer book with prayers for the ordinary and
    extraordinary moments in a child's life"-- Provided by publisher.
Identifiers: LCCN 2021058117 (print) | LCCN 2021058118 (ebook) | ISBN
    9781506468808 (hardcover) | ISBN 9781506471402 (ebook)
Subjects: LCSH: Christian children--Prayers and devotions--Juvenile
    literature.
Classification: LCC BV265 .S65 2022 (print) | LCC BV265 (ebook) | DDC
    242/.82--dc23/eng/20220112
LC record available at https://lccn.loc.gov/2021058117
LC ebook record available at https://lccn.loc.gov/2021058118

VN0004589; 9781506468808; JUL2022

Beaming Books
PO Box 1209
Minneapolis, MN 55440-1209
Beamingbooks.com

Little Prayers
for
EVERYDAY
LIFE

by **TRACI SMITH**

illustrated by **ANNA JONES**

MINNEAPOLIS

AUTHOR'S NOTE

Childhood is full of all sorts of ordinary and extraordinary moments that pass us by, sometimes much too quickly. *Little Prayers for Everyday Life* turns these moments into opportunities for brief prayer together. It's never too early to start to pray with your little one! The prayers in this book are written for you to pray with your child, and as they grow, they may start to repeat and memorize them. As you pray together, you are teaching your child how to pray.

Prayer is not a "one size fits all" part of family life. You can even add to the prayers or make up your own as you go. These prayers are a sort of canvas for you to paint as you wish. Enter into this journey with confidence and wonder, knowing that God has given you everything you need. Enjoy!

CONTENTS

MORNING

We thank you, God, for morning light
and peace and quiet through the night.
We thank you, God, for birds that sing.
We thank you, God, for everything.

MEALTIME

Here, at the table, we come to eat
and share God's love with all we meet.

For the food that we eat
and the love that we share,
thank you, God.

BATH TIME

As I'm splashing in the bath,
I wash my hands and feet and toes.
I thank God for my body,
how it moves and runs and grows.

GOD HEARS ME

God, you hear me when I pray.

Your love is never far away.

I can pray if I'm happy or lonely or sad.

I can pray when I'm tired or worried or mad.

I can pray every day and every season.

I can even pray without a reason!

SEASONS

Winter, spring, summer, fall:
God in heaven made them all.

The seasons change, the weather too.
But God's love for me is always true.

WELCOME BABY

God, we thank you for our newest
family member.

Please help us welcome the baby into
our family with hugs and kisses.

May we help when the baby cries or needs us.

May we smile when the baby makes us happy.

Thank you, God. Thank you!

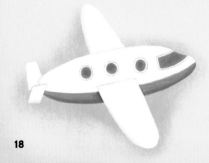

LOST TOOTH

I lost a tooth today, hooray!
It's a sign of how I grow.
My smile looks so strange to me,
Like someone I don't know!
I look at my reflection.
I smile wide and pray:
Thank you, God, for guiding me
each and every day.

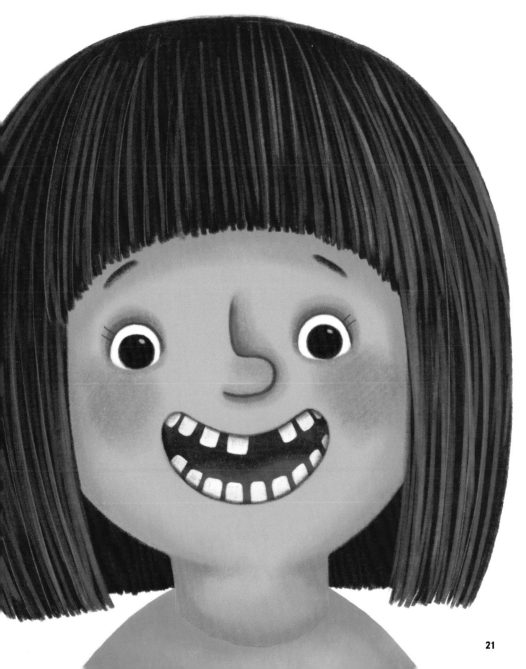

BE WITH ME TODAY

God, please be with me today
as I grow and learn and play.
Help me to know you are with me
each and every day.

BIRTHDAY

God, you know everything about me.

You know when I wake up and when I go to bed.

You even know how many hairs are on my head!

You knew me when I was a baby,

and you will know me when I am old.

You will always know me and love me.

Every year on my birthday I remember your love.

Happy birthday to me!

NEW PET

God, you made all the animals on the earth.

Some crawl. Some slither. Some fly.

Some have fur. Some have scales.
Some have feathers.

Today we give thanks for our new pet.

May our pet be a blessing to our family
and a new friend to love.

Help us treat our pet with love and respect.

May we care for our pet and show our love
every day.

I DID IT!

On this day, God, I shine, shine, shine!
I feel proud and so happy—
I did it!
When I do great things,
help me to remember this:
You love me when I do great things,
and you love me when I don't.
Your love is always there for me.
I don't have to earn it.

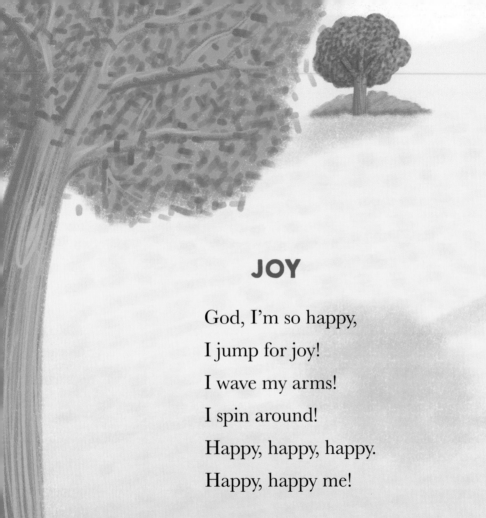

JOY

God, I'm so happy,

I jump for joy!

I wave my arms!

I spin around!

Happy, happy, happy.

Happy, happy me!

UPSET

God, I don't feel happy today.
I'm sad
or mad
or tired.
Be near to me as I breathe in
and breathe out.

I feel fresh air in my lungs.

I know these feelings won't last forever.

I pray they soon fade away.

In and out I breathe.

In and out I breathe.

Hard feelings don't last forever.

FEAR

When I am afraid, I trust.

I trust God. I trust my family. I trust myself.

BE STILL

Be still my heart,

be still.

Be still my mind,

be still.

Be still my feet. Be still my hands.

Be still,

be still,

be still.

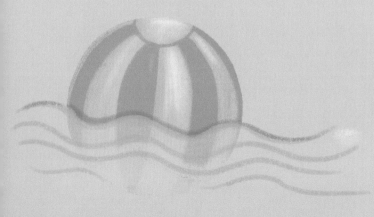

ILLNESS

Sometimes when I am sick,

I don't feel my best.

I lie down.

I sleep.

I take medicine.

Please help me feel better.

Give me comfort.

Give me rest.

Give me peace.

PEACE

Peace, peace, peace,
peace in our hearts,
peace.
Peace in our minds,
peace.
Peace when we wake,
peace when we sleep,
peace shining bright in our lives.

MAY PEACE PREVAIL ON EARTH

DIFFICULT NEWS

God, when sad things happen,
you are sad too.

You understand.

Thank you, God,
for always hearing us.

Help us to be kind and peaceful, always.

We light a candle to remind us
of your love for all.

A PRAYER FOR EVERY DAY

God, you love me all the time.
All the time, I am your child.

GOODNIGHT

I stretch up high.
I bend down low.
I hug the ones I love.

Goodnight, family.
Goodnight, world.
Goodnight, God!

BEDTIME

At night we stop. We go to bed.

We rest our bodies. We rest our heads.

We say good night. The day is done.

We pray God's peace for everyone.

ABOUT THE AUTHOR
AND ILLUSTRATOR

TRACI SMITH is an ordained minister, mother of three, and author. Traci's passion is helping families find times for connection and spiritual nourishment amid the hustle and bustle of daily life. What began as a quest to help her own family has provided valuable insight for thousands of others. She is the author of several books including *Prayers for Faithful Families: Everyday Prayers for Everyday Life*, *Faithful Families: Creating Sacred Moments at Home*, and *When Kids Ask Hard Questions: Faith-Filled Responses for Tough Topics*. Traci believes faith practices should be fun, easy to fit into daily life, and accessible to all. Visit her at traci-smith.com.

ANNA JONES has been illustrating children's books since 2010, and her work has been published in the UK, the US, The Netherlands, Korea, and South America. She lives in Edinburgh, Scotland.